EDUCATION LIBRARY SERVICE

Tel: 01606 275801

Cheshire West
and Chester

Cheshire East
Council

THE YOUNG ENTREPRENEURS' CLUB
COMMUNICATIONS

MIKE HOBBS

W
FRANKLIN WATTS
LONDON • SYDNEY

First published in 2013 by Franklin Watts

Copyright © Franklin Watts 2013
Franklin Watts
338 Euston Road
London NW1 3BH

Franklin Watts Australia
Level 17/207 Kent Street
Sydney, NSW 2000

Series Editor: Paul Rockett
Editor: Hayley Fairhead
Consultant: David Gray
Design: Simon Borrough
Picture Research: Diana Morris

Dewey number: 791'.069

ISBN: 978 1 4451 1398 2

Printed in China

Franklin Watts is a division of
Hachette Children's Books,
an Hachette UK company.

www.hachette.co.uk

Picture credits: T Anderson/Shutterstock, 12r;
www.automattic.com, 37t; badahos/istockphoto,
8b; www.bangbang-films.com, 21; http://bu.mp, 27;
Colorlife/Shutterstock, front cover inset; Araya Diaz/
Getty Images, 17b; Empire 331/Dreamstime, 38;
felinda/istockphoto, 30; fkdkondmi/Shutterstock,
18t; www.grasshopper.com, 19; www.groupme.
com, 41; Izabela Habur/Getty Images, 14;
http://hearsaysocial.com, 29; Jonathan Hordle/
Rex Features, 25t; Roger Jegg Fotodesign.de/
Shutterstock, 10; Courtney Keating/istockphoto, 24;
Chris Lobina /Rex Features, 12bl; Saul Loeb/AFP/
Getty Images, 17t; Artem Loskutnikov/Shutterstock,
8bg; Oleksly Maksymenko/Alamy, 33; Artur
Marciniec/istockphoto, 40b; www.mashable.com,
31b; M4OSPhotos/Alamy, 11b; Gary Miller/Getty
Images, 31t; Monkey Business Images/Dreamstime,
28; Mikkel William Nielson/istockphoto, 36;
www.nokia.com, 39; nyul/istockphoto, 16;
www.onswipe.com, 13; Ponsuwan/Shutterstock,
15l; Pali Rao/istockphoto, 26; Rex Features, 23t;
Michael Rubin/Shutterstock, 34; Nadine Rupp /Getty
Images, 11t; sitade/ istockphoto, 40t; Lee Snider/
Dreamstime, 35; Cameron Spencer/Getty Images,
7; Stocklife/Shutterstock, 5; Summly, 23b; Charles
Sykes/Rex Features, 25b; www.theappfactory.
co.uk, 15t, 15c;   Times Newspapers/Rex Features,:
9t; Bruno Toldi/istockphoto, front cover bg; Sunny
S Unal/Corbis Flirt/Alamy, 22; Vectorstudio/
Shutterstock, 20; Jim West/Alamy, 32;
www.wordpress.com, 37b; 0833379753/
Shutterstock, 18b.

CONTENTS

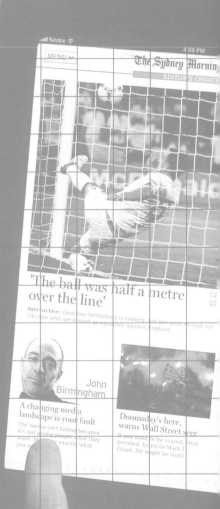

The communications world

Speeding up the process

The communications world is all about the way we receive information: from new media to traditional media. New media includes the Internet (social network sites and blogs), mobile phones and apps. Traditional media includes TV, radio, newspapers and magazines. There are also methods of business communications, such as advertising and public relations. The massive growth of Internet and smartphone usage is leading to fewer readers of books and newspapers worldwide. TV and radio audiences are not increasing, except in certain countries.

Therefore, if you're interested in becoming a communications entrepreneur, it seems to make sense for you to look at new media. How can you help deliver information to smartphones and PCs faster and more reliably, whilst making a profit? There is still a place for traditional forms of communication. You might even have an idea that transforms their use.

CHALLENGE

Think of two new media ideas and two traditional media ideas that might interest you.

Inspiring entrepreneur
Gordon Roddick

A good entrepreneur moves with the times from traditional to new media, and Gordon Roddick (above) is proof of this. He co-founded *The Big Issue*, a weekly magazine produced and sold in the UK by the homeless, selling 300,000 copies at the height of its success in 2001. He went on to set up 38 Degrees with Henry Tinsley (of Green & Black's chocolate). 38 Degrees is a not-for-profit online campaigning group which relies on donations from members to fund its work.

Gordon Roddick is a social entrepreneur. As with all entrepreneurs, he invests his time, money and effort into developing an idea, but with the aim of benefiting society rather than just making a profit. The campaigns which 38 Degrees launches are chosen by the group's members. The group's main successes include campaigns against selling off forestry land in the UK, supporting fights against cuts within the BBC and the National Health Service and raising awareness about climate change.

YOUR THOUGHTS

Do you think that the Internet is the best form of new media to raise awareness about 38 Degrees' campaigns? Explain your answer.

The secrets of entrepreneurship

Have you got what it takes?

An entrepreneur is a person who takes a financial risk to bring a new idea to market. As an entrepreneur you will invest time, money and energy in developing an idea with the aim of making a profit. It will involve plenty of hard work, although it can be incredibly rewarding. There is no single way to succeed, but there are certain important qualities you must have.

You must have a good knowledge of the communications market, the products available and where new services or inventions could make a difference. You must have plenty of enthusiasm and energy in order to keep yourself going even when business is difficult. You should be hard-working, able to make good business choices have a sound knowledge media technology. Above all, you should have a burning passion to that your idea becomes successful.

CHALLENGE

Looking at the ideas you noted down from page 8, is there one that you are especially passionate about? Think of reasons why.

Young entrepreneur

Tumblr

David Karp (left) of New York City, USA, showed the vision, enterprise and drive to set up and grow his company. Tumblr is a social networking service which provides a platform for bloggers to post short, mixed media messages. The site's selling point is that it's incredibly simple to use. It has proved massively popular for people aged under 25. It now has over 36 million followers and is adding users at the rate of 750,000 per month.

David's vision was that bloggers would be happy to update their blogs more often if it was made easier for them to do so. David was 21 when he founded Tumblr using the money he had earned as a software consultant. The mixed media microblogs (containing pictures, film and music) are known as tumblelogs. Celebrities who have used the site range from Lady Gaga to President Obama. Eighty-five per cent of users update their blogs at least twenty times a month, whereas previously less than 10 per cent had updated within the last four months. David was named Best Young Tech Entrepreneur by *Businessweek* in 2009.

YOUR THOUGHTS

What entrepreneurial qualities did David show in getting Tumblr going?

Can your ideas make a difference?

Testing time

As someone really interested in communications, you're probably bursting with ideas about what you might like to do. It's important that you concentrate on one product or service and choose wisely. Get advice from wherever you can, including friends and family. But it's your decision. You must love your chosen idea, whether it be a new smartphone app or a new PR company.

If you've chosen a new media idea you should test your product or service first. Perhaps, for instance, it's an app for country walks in your area. Now you need to discover whether it will work. It must be reliable and easy to use. Try it out on some members of the public. You could either set up a formal user group or get some friends to try the application for free. You should test it under all conditions and try every possible sequence to find out whether you've got something you can develop. Only then will you know whether your idea might truly work.

CHALLENGE

You have produced an app for country walks. You are now going to test it. What three things do you want it to do?

Onswipe

Young entrepreneurs
Onswipe

Andres Barreto (right), 24, and Jason Baptiste (below), 25, of Miami, Florida, USA, came up with and developed their ideas for Onswipe in early 2011, around the time the iPad came out. Andres and Jason wanted to develop a plug-in which could make improvements to how things looked on the tablet very quickly. During their testing they realised that websites and blogs were not built for touch and swipe technology like apps were. So, they developed a plug-in with the all-important touch technology.

Onswipe makes all content look fantastic on tablet devices in a very short time, which is important in such a fast moving market. With the rapid growth of iPad use, Onswipe was definitely an idea for the moment. 'Insanely easy tablet publishing' is what they call it, and it's free to use (the company makes its money from advertising). Onswipe received $1 million in start-up funds at the beginning of 2011 with a further $5 million from backers a few months later.

YOUR THOUGHTS

Do you think Andres and Jason hit on a good idea with Onswipe once they had finished testing? Is it something you would use?

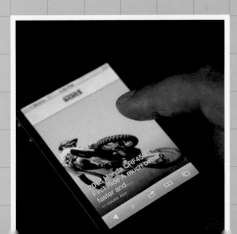

Conducting your market research

Primary and secondary research

Well, your product or service works well, but are there going to be enough people who might actually want to buy and use your product or service? Turning a good idea into a profitable one means you must discover whether there's a market for it. You should research your potential market properly before you go any further. Market research is divided into two different types:

Primary research – information you gather for the first time from direct observation or questions to the public;
Secondary research – information already collected that you can find from sources such as the Internet or the library.

There are plenty of ways you can get feedback about whether you're onto a winning idea. Perhaps you've plans for a magazine about teenage fashion, in which case you might start asking people whether they read this type of magazine regularly. You could go to your town's shopping centre to find out. Maybe you can get some of your friends to help you. When you add the results of these first-hand responses to the knowledge you've gained from your secondary research (discussion with newsagents, visits to libraries), you should have a clear picture of the market.

CHALLENGE

Think of four questions you could ask members of the public about your potential fashion magazine.

Young entrepreneur
The App Factory

David Carter (left) of Manchester, UK, was just 18 when he launched his company, The App Factory, in 2010. He had looked into the app market by doing primary research on successful apps and asking the public why they worked. He had also carried out some secondary research on overall numbers of app downloads before deciding that The App Factory, which develops general and specific mobile applications, could have a future.

David's business builds apps for all the main platforms and devices and has developed over 70 specific apps for Android. For his primary research he downloaded and used all the most popular apps on all the mobile platforms and got a feel for why they were proving to be hits. Although the actual costs for each individual app download are small (typically, say, £0.99 or $0.99), he realised that a good number of sales would soon make the numbers add up. The success of The App Factory has led David to found The Corporate Group for which he is Chief Executive Officer.

YOUR THOUGHTS

What other primary and secondary research could David have carried out?

Getting the money together

Finding start-up funds

Once you have your idea and know your market, you need money to get you started. Explore every avenue to find some funds, from family and friends to banks, investors and government grants. There may well be special grants for young entrepreneurs in your area: check online or in libraries to see if these apply to you. The people who lend you the money are generally called backers. In nearly all cases, they will want you to agree to give something in return for funding you.

Let's say you've decided to set up a public relations company that works for good causes. You will stand more chance of securing investment if you've got a proper financial plan (see page 24), showing what these backers will get in return and when they'll get it. Investors need to know how long it will take for them to be repaid, so be as realistic as you can.

CHALLENGE

You've got an idea for a communications business. Which three sources would you first approach for start-up funds?

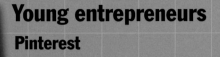

Young entrepreneurs

Pinterest

Ben Silbermann (right) and Paul Sciarra from Iowa, USA, started to develop their company, Pinterest, in 2009, when they were in their late twenties. Pinterest is a pinboard-style photo-sharing website where people can post images of their favourite things. They were able to convince investors of the many uses of their 'photo pin' idea so as to raise enough capital for their start-up fund. From this, Pinterest was launched in early 2010. Progress was a little slow at first: by the end of the year the site only had 11,000 users.

Nevertheless, the founders kept going. They hired designer Evan Sharp (left) as a co-founder and launched a Pinterest iPhone app in early 2011 to great reviews. After the app's success, Pinterest received $10 million in development funding. A further investment $27 million in October 2011 saw growth continue to rise. By January 2012, the site had 11.7 million users. Further investment of $120 million means Pinterest is now valued at $1.5 billion.

YOUR THOUGHTS

At which stage of the company's development would you have invested money? Explain your answer.

Spending time on product development

Finding out what works

Once you've secured some funding, you need to start developing your product. In a fast-moving world such as communications, you must constantly check that your idea remains ahead of the game. Your product could be a mobile phone that answers calls when you speak anywhere near the mouthpiece. It needs to look good with a clean and uncomplicated design. You'd need to develop a way of ensuring it responds to your voice alone.

After your earlier research, you should have a pretty good understanding of what will work and what won't. You need to keep improving your idea so that it is faster, looks better and meets the needs of the user. For instance, would there be a problem with you answering calls without realising? You've got to be confident in its function. Online applications don't go live all at once but in stages, to find out where the problems are. Your product can be developed in the light of this experience. The time spent in development is absolutely vital.

CHALLENGE

If you were going to develop a voice-sensitive mobile phone, what main features would you look at?

Young entrepreneurs
Grasshopper

David Hauser (right) and Siamak Taghaddos (left) of Needham, Massachusetts, USA, developed a service which provides virtual phone systems for small businesses. With their company, Grasshopper, you can make your start-up company appear to have all the different office functions (production, marketing, sales, distribution, finance) through one simple phone hub. When they started in 2003 that was just what David and Siamak (both then in their early twenties) knew their small business needed.

Grasshopper®
The Entrepreneur's Phone System

YOUR THOUGHTS

Do you think the Grasshopper team chose a good name for their virtual phone system? Can you suggest another name, and why would it be suitable?

The ability to develop their original ideas, including a change of name (the original name, GotVMail, just didn't sound so snappy), managed to give their company the greatest chance of success. David and Siamak aimed to make entrepreneurs sound more professional and stay connected from anywhere. They have developed lots of features including customised greetings and the ability to forward calls to anywhere in the world. Today, they have over 30,000 clients and have won many awards, including being named one of *Businessweek's* Top Five Entrepreneurs Under 25.

Do you have any rivals?

Checking out the competition

Unfortunately, no matter how good your idea, you are always likely to face some competition. This may be either direct competition from businesses selling similar products, or from rivals chasing the same customers. You'll be really keen to get going by now, but there's still one last vital piece of research you have to do. Who are you up against?

Let's say that you are developing an app as part of your fashion magazine idea. You would need to find out if anyone else is working on the same idea. In all probability they are, and they may even have launched their product. But don't give up. Look carefully at what your direct competitors are doing. See what's good about them, what's not so good, and learn from both. There may well be flaws in their design, which you can overcome. It's not always about being first to market (though it helps): it's about being better than your rivals. Always think about how you will make your idea stand out from the crowd.

CHALLENGE

Look at four fashion magazine apps and rate them for their design, the things they can do, their reliability and ease of use. How could you make your app better?

Young entrepreneur
Bang Bang Films

Roopak Saluja of Mumbai, India, was 30 when he set up his advertising business, Bang Bang Films. His company has outstripped its rivals as an international force in TV and film advertising, and he has set up a sister business, Jack in the Box Worldwide, which focuses especially on advertising in new media.

YOUR THOUGHTS

Do you think Roopak was right to take on the competition both in India and worldwide? Why?

Roopak had worked in advertising for several years and had noticed that the Indian film and media industry only focused on Indian projects. So he believed he would have few Indian rivals when his company made pitches to work outside India. He would also be the first in India to call on directors from the USA and Europe as well as Indian talent, giving him a competitive advantage. Naturally, it has taken time, and his companies still have most of their work in Asian-Pacific and Middle Eastern countries, but his analysis and strategy have proved successful.

Using new technological breakthroughs

Taking the lead

Communications is one of the main areas where a small technological innovation can make all the difference between success and failure. Breakthroughs are happening very fast these days, and if you've created a technological advantage (or you're responsible as the entrepreneur for marketing one), then this will increase your chances of success. Your task is to make this technology part of your product in lightning speed. Even if you've done a lot of work on your previous model, you can't afford to ignore such a breakthrough.

Communications technology is always advancing. Apps have constant upgrades and new smartphones come onto the market with increasing speed. Technological improvements can add power to your marketing campaign and can provide key selling points to get ahead of the competition.

▼ **Advances in mobile phone technology mean that people can communicate at any time, whatever they are doing.**

CHALLENGE

Can you think of three recent technological breakthroughs in communications and how they've helped us in our lives?

Young entrepreneur
Summly

Nick D'Aloisio of London, UK, was a schoolboy barely into his teens when he invented an app that would help people search more precisely for the information they needed online. He did this by putting search results into clear categories and used that technological advantage to enable his company, Summly, to receive terrific publicity. Following on from that, he was able to raise money from San Francisco's Horizon Ventures followed by further investment from Hong Kong billionaire, Li Ka-shing.

Obviously, search engines have been around for almost as long as the Internet. But Nick used algorithms to achieve a technological breakthrough. His app, which was at first called Trimit, is able to detect different topics on webpages. These differences in turn trigger different responses which give a much clearer idea of the content to the user. Launched in December 2011, Summly gained over 100,000 downloads in its first month, and was soon named the UK's App of the Week by Apple.

YOUR THOUGHTS

Would Nick have been given the same funding without his technological breakthrough? Give reasons for your answer.

Making a financial plan

Where the money goes

Once you start to get near to bringing your product or service to the marketplace, you must make proper financial plans for it to make money as soon as possible. You'll find that the costs are starting to go up and up. You may have to start paying for office furniture, PCs, phones, heat and light, not to mention any people who you bring in to help. Show how your costs are going to be covered by projected sales. Make sure you're adding in all the little items associated with your business, however unrelated they may seem.

Some of the details that would appear in the plan include:

- Amount you need to invest;
- Amount you'll pay on weekly running costs;
- Other estimated costs;
- Predicted sales for your first year.

Once you're in business with a planned budget, the two important things to remember are profit and cash flow. Remember, you must make a profit if you want to stay in business. You also need to see that cash is coming in regularly. Try to arrange for fees to be paid each month. In difficult economic times, the largest cause of company failure is late payments and unpaid bills.

CHALLENGE

You want to ask a bank or some backers for a loan to get your business started. Think about what your running costs and other estimated costs may be.

Young entrepreneurs
Twitter

Everybody is now familiar with the concept of tweets (short public messages with a maximum of 140 characters) which are put up on the platform of Twitter. Jack Dorsey (below), Biz Stone and Evan Williams of San Francisco, USA, founded Twitter in 2006. They were able to bring in funding even before money was coming into the company because of their predicted sales. They were able to show backers that interest in the microblog and social networking would inevitably lead to huge use of Twitter. So they raised roughly $60 million in three stages: an initial sum of about $3 million, followed by second and third stage funding of $22 million then $35 million.

Since then, further capital of $200 million has been raised along with an investment of $800 million from backers. The investors are buying into a huge user group: Twitter has well over 100 million users, growing at over 300,000 each day. Twitter's revenue is also growing fast. It had almost doubled within a year to $260 million by the end of 2012.

YOUR THOUGHTS

Do you think the Twitter backers were wise to invest in the social media site's potential?

Putting together a strong team

Picking people carefully

It's very unlikely you'll be able to do everything yourself, no matter how much of a super salesman or techno-whiz you are. You'll have to bring in a supporting team of people you can trust. This will include people experienced in accounts and administration, as well as others who are going to help you find new business and handle the clients and the media. You might ask someone with recruitment experience to help you, if you have not interviewed and selected before.

Once you've brought in the right people, you're only halfway there. Now you must create a team. Teamwork is vital, especially in the communications field, where so many businesses involve people with different skills getting together. Your first priority is to encourage them to work together as a tight unit, communicating closely and listening to what they each have to say. Getting this to happen will require some good leadership from you.

CHALLENGE

You're recruiting for your company. Which two questions would you ask people?

Young entrepreneurs
Bump Technologies

David Lieb (middle), Jake Mintz (right) and Andy Huibers (left) built up Bump Technologies of San Francisco, California, USA, by bringing in the right people to help their company to grow through a series of contacts and interviews. The enlarged team has been able to boost the impact of their Bump device, a free app which transmits contact information from one iPhone, iPad or Android to another. Through licensing fees and transaction fees (Bump is used by PayPal for people to transfer funds) the company is bringing in money as well as boosting its customer base.

David, Jake and Andy launched Bump in 2009 when they were all in their twenties and rapidly started to get noticed (being the billionth app downloaded from Apple's store helped). As a result, they soon had to start bringing in people to help them. With investment from venture capital funds and Google, they have been able to grow, carefully selecting people with similar goals. They needed clever, talented designers and developers who all shared the aim of changing the way people use their mobile phones. They now have 21 people working for them.

YOUR THOUGHTS

Do you think it was important that the Bump founders brought in people with similar interests? What might have happened otherwise?

Guiding everyone in the right direction

Becoming used to leadership

There are many different types of leader and there are lots of different skills you need to be a good leader – but, as a budding entrepreneur, you'll have to discover a style that's right for you and your business. You might choose to have others making certain decisions, yet you'll still want everyone working for the same goals. Let's say you've invented a new app for comparing trainers and it is getting close to launch. How many trainer brands do you include? Which towns and cities do you focus on? You must always listen to advice from others who may have more experience than you, but it is likely that you will be making the final decisions.

This isn't something that anyone will expect you to learn overnight. It takes time and practice. A few mistakes are forgivable in the early days as you pick up problem-solving skills. When you're tackling a problem, it's up to you to see the big picture. You need to look at the short- and long-term effects of any decisions you make.

CHALLENGE

Taking the example of the new trainers app, what is your overall focus? Should you concentrate on a few trainers you think are best or put out information about as many trainers as you can?

Young entrepreneurs
Hearsay Social

Clara Shih (below) and Steve Garrity (right) of San Francisco, California, USA, set up Hearsay Social in 2011. The company provides technology which helps big businesses communicate directly with local customers using social media. They saw that national companies needed to manage social media pages (Twitter, Facebook) to make sure they had close links with all their different local branches and customers. Their social media idea has become the way businesses discover what people are saying about them.

The leadership style at Hearsay Social is relaxed and fun. The focus is on brainstorming, giving advice and working closely together. There are no private offices, just meeting rooms for sharing ideas. The offices are sunny and open-plan; and they even have a sound system to provide a soundtrack to their working day!

YOUR THOUGHTS

Do you think Hearsay Social's leadership style has contributed to its success?

Working out a marketing plan

Building your customer base

You'll have to develop a strong marketing plan as the day for your launch approaches. Do all you can to sell as much of your product or service as fast as possible, making sure that new and traditional media are buzzing with news of your launch. Work out your marketing plan, adding in all the different parts of the marketing mix – and make sure your plan is linked to the budget you prepared earlier.

Once you've decided on your plan, you need to put it into action. To do this, it's often helpful to think of the four Ps:

Product – what your product offers and what sets it apart from its competition (are there any similar apps?).

Price – what your customers will be prepared to pay (do you have a special introductory price?).

Place – how and where you are going to sell your product – in shops, supermarkets, online or all three?

Promotion – how to reach your market most effectively. This can include advertising, PR, direct mail and personal selling.

CHALLENGE

Using the four Ps, put down the main marketing plan principles you'd follow to get the best sales for your new trainers app.

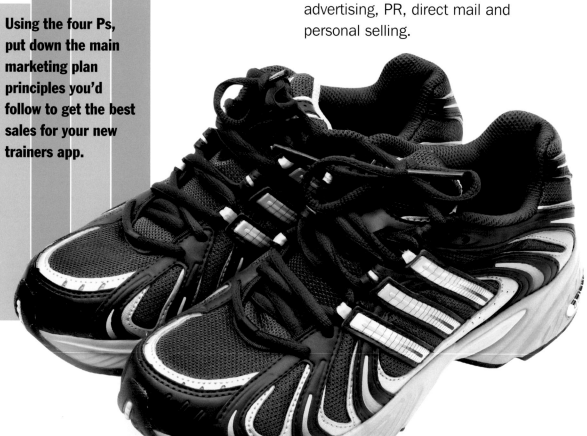

Young entrepreneur
Mashable

Pete Cashmore (left), originally from Aberdeen, UK, developed his blog network, Mashable, when he was 19. Now based in New York City and San Francisco, California, USA, Pete has developed Mashable into a website for all those who want easily understandable information to keep up with social media and new technology.

Pete's idea was to make all the important information on new technology and social media updates available through a series of short, punchy pieces of information. His marketing plan was to target all users, both technical and non-technical. He made his site clear and straightforward but also smart enough to appeal to those in the know, and advertised on social media sites like Twitter. The network now has 20 million users and 6 million regular followers.

YOUR THOUGHTS

Do you think product or the means of promoting it was most important for Pete, and why?

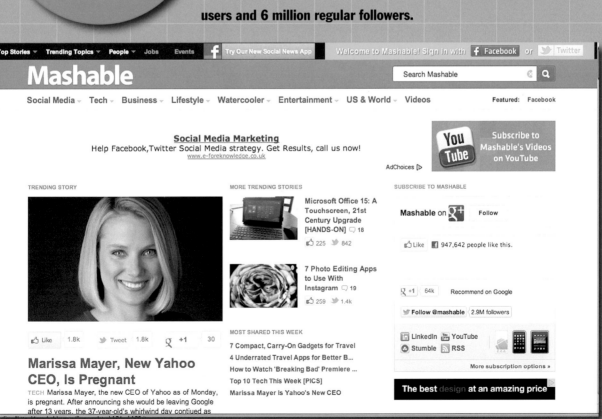

Gaining publicity

Telling people your great plans

You'll have to draw up a programme that makes sure your target market hears about what you are offering. It doesn't matter how good your product is if no-one has heard about it. And if you're launching an online site, are your target customers aware of what you're doing?

Two of the main ways of letting people know are advertising and public relations. Advertising aims to get your product in the right media to grab your customers' attention. Publicity means using events or promotions to put your name in the public eye. You can use a mixture of PR, social media networking, TV, newspaper and radio advertising to get the word out. Plan any advertising campaign you can afford with great care, and support it with other promotional work. Free trials, sales promotions, samples and other incentives are all ways of showing your product in the best light.

CHALLENGE

To gain publicity for an idea, such as a new local radio station, would you focus on social media networks or traditional media? Why?

▼ **Holding a press conference is a great way to launch a new product.**

Young entrepreneur

Bizoogo

Erez Nounou of London, UK, is going about the business of publicising his new start-up company, Bizoogo, in a very modern way. Bizoogo is a social media network which helps different entrepreneurs and business advisors to come together and start up new businesses. Founded in early 2012 when Erez was 27, Bizoogo is a much-needed communications tool for entrepreneurs with new business ideas.

He is using social media to spread the news about his company. Erez writes his own blog and uses Facebook, Twitter and LinkedIn. He admits that he is fortunate to be starting at a time when so many people are already online, giving him the chance to publicise Bizoogo for very little money. Erez is using his growing online community to get his message across.

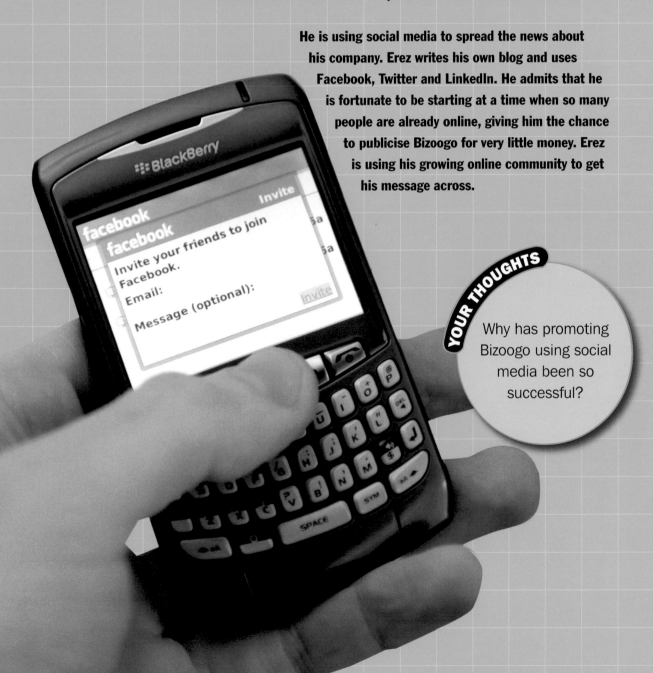

YOUR THOUGHTS

Why has promoting Bizoogo using social media been so successful?

Out into the world

Launching your business

The long wait is over at last. You're launching today and suddenly everything is happening at once. Just make sure you do everything you can to get a good start. It's time to focus all your attention on your big launch. One obvious way to get some press and social media coverage is to throw a party, but don't let your message get lost in all the fun. You don't want all your hard work and planning to go to waste. A party might make a good splash but it is the demonstrations that will prove really useful, so people can see what your product actually does.

In fact, your launch is a very good chance to communicate with your target audience. Create as big a noise as you can, and make sure you keep up the energy and momentum. You'll want reviews and feedback from blogs, Facebook, Twitter, radio, TV, newspapers and magazines. They won't all love your idea straightaway, however, unless you're very lucky. Just be happy they're commenting on your project.

CHALLENGE

Think of a theme that would make the launch party of your voice-sensitive mobile phone memorable.

Meet iPad
...volutionary product at an unbelievable price.

Meet iPad
A magical and revolutionary product at an unbelievable price.

Young entrepreneur
ADstruc

John Laramie of New York City, USA, launched ADstruc in summer 2010. He had worked in the outdoor advertising industry (e.g. posters and digital displays outdoors) and believed it was slow and old-fashioned. John, who was 25 at the time, designed ADstruc, a service which brought all the buying, selling and positioning of outdoor advertising together online. ADstruc aimed to make the business of outdoor advertising quicker and more profitable for everyone.

Shows and fairs make excellent places to launch. ADstruc launched at Techstars' Investor Day, showing the company's technological edge and attracting important customers and investors. Since launching, ADstruc now has 700 advertisers who use the site to find the billboards they want to advertise on.

YOUR THOUGHTS

Why do you think John's launch was successful?

Keep on looking to improve

▶ **Phone manufacturers saw the opportunity to increase their market with smartphones that can make live video calls.**

Checking sales and distribution

Once everything is up and running, you shouldn't sit back – instead, keep looking for opportunities where you can sell to more customers. Is there really a large enough market for your company to be successful? It's never too late to make changes. Say you launched a voice-recognition mobile phone. Is it really going to help people when they are driving for instance? Could you tie in with car dealers and manufacturers? Might your voice-recognition phone help the blind in some way?

CHALLENGE

List six different shops or outlets where you might sell your new app or blog.

If you've launched a product, such as an online app for comparing new trainers, and you're selling through certain sites, are they the right sites for the type of people who might buy? You always need to check whether you're reaching your target market. You may do better if you only sell your product through your own site. The important thing is that you make any adjustments as fast as you can.

Young entrepreneur
Automattic

Matthew Mullenweg (left) and Ryan Boren of San Francisco, California, USA, developed their free communication tool and blog, WordPress.com, in 2005, using their special blogging software. They were both in their early twenties at the time. The software and blog were both instant successes and later that year Automattic was founded to run the WordPress business. Automattic charges users for upgrades to their blog, such as anti-spam technology. By early 2006, they were able to raise $1.1 million to help grow their services. A series of awards have helped to keep sales rising.

By July 2011, the software was powering over 50 million blogs and by April 2012, the WordPress blog was one of the top 100 most followed blogs. Meanwhile Matt and Ryan have used the WordPress success to help increase the sales of other inventions from their company. These inventions include Akismet (anti-spam software), Gravatar (globally recognised avatars), and VaultPress (backup and security). While none have been as successful as WordPress, they have all helped to boost the company's profits.

AUTOMATTIC

YOUR THOUGHTS

Do you believe the Automattic guys were right to introduce new services rather than concentrate solely on WordPress? If so, why?

Password | Log In | ☑ Remember me | Forgot password? | **Sign Up**

 WORDPRESS.COM

A better way to blog.

Get started here

Learn more or sign up now.

Freshly Pressed:

The best of **437,865** bloggers, **1,172,495** new posts, **1,506,321** comments, & **258,052,155** words posted today on WordPress.com.

Berlin Tempelhof – Playground Airport
ciapannaphoto
Posts about Photography →

The Limitations of 'Like'
Stuff Worth Talking About

Wandering the Streets of Seoul's University District
brynacaroline

In the Summertime, I Read Books
BookPeople's Blog

A Guide to Packing Light
The Squeaky Robot
Posts about Travel →

INADIFFERENTVOICE

Setbacks can be useful

Turning problems into opportunities

You're bound to have problems, because everyone does when they're trying to run a business. Think about things logically, and you should be able to come up with an answer. Often when you come up with a solution to a problem, you'll see that it's actually taken you onto a new track that will help your business to grow even faster.

For example, let's say that your app which alerts people to great new TV programmes has been successful until people start complaining that they can't gain access to the app in certain areas. Obviously there's nothing you can do about the mobile phone signals themselves, but it may get you thinking about another app that you could market in addition to it. And this could become a new opportunity…

CHALLENGE

When a problem crops up with an app you have developed, would you think about withdrawing it from the market to fix it? Why?

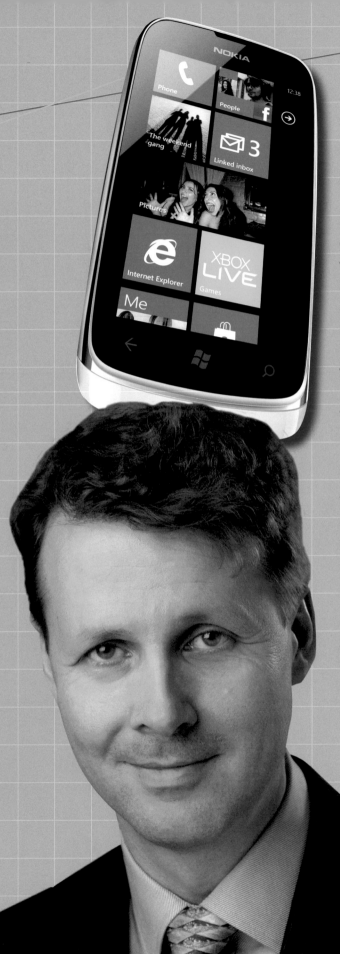

Inspiring entrepreneur
Risto Siilasmaa

Until recently, Nokia was the largest mobile phone company in the world. The Finnish company took over the number one spot from Motorola in 1999. In 2008, its worldwide market share was a staggering 41 per cent but when smartphones, such as Apple's iPhone and the Google Android, came on the market, that share began to decline fast. By 2012, it had almost halved and the Korean company Samsung (which had reacted quicker to market changes) had taken over the leading position.

So, Nokia definitely had a problem and they looked to entrepreneur, Risto Siilasmaa (left), for help. Risto made his name by creating the successful anti-virus software F-Secure. His was the first company to sell anti-virus software on the Internet. He was appointed Chairman of Nokia in May 2012 (he had been on the board learning about the business since 2008). Risto says that it is his aim to add entrepreneurial thinking to Nokia. Perhaps he will be able to ensure that the setback suffered by the company turns into an opportunity.

YOUR THOUGHTS

Why do you think entrepreneurial thinking can be good for a large, established company like Nokia?

So what's next?

Building on your success

As soon as you've achieved the goals you set yourself, the smart thing is to be planning your next move. People (colleagues, investors, customers) will be even more interested in your ideas, now the first one has been a success. This is the time when real entrepreneurs look to grow their success by expanding their business. And once you've experienced the thrill of making one business a hit, you'll probably want to do it all over again.

How can you best do this? There should be a natural link between the ideas you have, although it's not essential. For instance, your computer games PR business might offer you a chance to become involved in developing a potentially successful new computer game. It's up to you.

CHALLENGE

Write down a follow-up plan for your own business idea.

▲ Your voice-recognition phone might give you the idea of inventing a similar TV remote control.

Young entrepreneurs
GroupMe

Jared Hecht (top), 23, and Steve Martocci (below), 28, of New York City, USA, first developed GroupMe, their group text messaging app, in 2010 so people could stay in touch at festivals and large concerts. They found that email connections were often lost in those places and phone calls only reached one person in the group. They needed something reliable which could be sent to more than one person at a time – group text messaging. They soon found out that people were keen to use their communications tool for all sorts of small personal social networks, and they began passing millions of messages every day.

GroupMe has become so successful so quickly that it was bought by the large communications company Skype for roughly $85 million in August 2011. Now their plans involve using the resources of Skype to develop GroupMe in many ways, such as Experiences by GroupMe, a new way to plan events with your friends.

YOUR THOUGHTS

What would you plan next if you were the GroupMe founders?

Glossary

advertising Images or stories that interest people in your product.

algorithms Logical arithmetical solutions to a particular set of problems.

applications (apps) Useful gadgets you download to your mobile phone.

avatars Pictures of the users, or their characters, in graphical form.

backers People who lend you money to help you start your business.

billboards Large outdoor boards used to display advertising posters.

blogs (short for web logs) Information or discussion sites on the Internet, updated regularly.

budget The amount of money you expect to spend (and receive).

cash flow The money coming in and going out.

costs Everything you must spend to make sales.

financial plan Estimate of how much money you need and how much you'll make.

invest To put money into a (new) business.

launch The moment you open your business or start selling your product.

market research Finding out if there's a market for your idea, or how it's doing.

market share The amount of sales you make compared to the complete market.

marketing mix The things you must do to market your goods.

marketing plan Describing your likely customers and how you'll sell to them.

new media Digital content that anyone can access and interact with e.g. the Internet.

phone hub The central point around which connected phones are linked.

product Anything that you make or produce for consumers to buy.

product development All the work done in getting your product ready to sell.

profit The amount of money you receive for sales, less the cost of making them.

publicity The ways you get your business noticed in the media.

public relations (PR) The work you do to give yourself a good reputation.

revenue All the money that comes into your business.

rivals Everyone who is competing with you to sell to consumers.

smartphone A mobile phone with advanced connecting features and computing ability.

social networking sites Websites that help you connect to other people.

start-up funds The money you need to find to begin to run your business.

target market The people you want to interest in buying your products.

traditional media Newspapers, magazines, TV, radio and books.

user group A special group set up to test a particular product.

venture capital Money that is invested in a new business in order to make a profit.

Further information

Websites of featured entrepreneurs

ADstruc **http://adstruc.com**
Automattic **http://automattic.com**
Bang Bang Films **http://bangbang-films.com**
Bizoogo **www.bizoogo.com**
Bump Technologies **https://bu.mp/**
Gordon Roddick **www.38degrees.org.uk**
Grasshopper **http://grasshopper.com**
GroupMe **https://groupme.com**
Hearsay Social **http://hearsaysocial.com**

Mashable **http://mashable.com**
Onswipe **http://onswipe.com**
Pinterest **www.pinterest.com**
Risto Siilasmaa **www.nokia.com/Official**
Summly **www.crunchbase.com/company/summly**
The App Factory **www.theappfactory.co.uk**
Tumblr **www.tumblr.com**
Twitter **https://twitter.com**

Other websites

www.bbc.co.uk/dragonsden/
Offical website of the *Dragon's Den* programme, where you can see other budding entrepreneurs and the advice they receive.

www.bbc.co.uk/youngapprentice
Official website of the *Young Apprentice* series, where youngsters try out their skills to succeed in business.

www.youngentrepreneur.com/
Online forum for information and advice on being a young entrepreneur.

Books

Everyday Inventions: Get the Message by Jane Bidder (Franklin Watts, 2009)
Media Power: Causes and Campaigns by Jenny Vaughan (Franklin Watts, 2009)
The Quick Expert's Guide: Building Your Own Website (Wayland, 2012)

Note to parents and teachers: every effort has been made by the publishers to ensure that these websites are suitable for children, and that they contain no inappropriate or offensive material. However, because of the nature of the Internet, it is impossible to guarantee that the contents of these sites will not be altered.

Index